THE THINGS WE SAY TO EACH OTHER

THE THINGS WE SAY TO EACH OTHER

Stephanie Jones

A look at emotional impulses, responses and their effects.

This is a work of fiction. Names, characters, places, and incidents either are the product of the author's imagination or are used fictitiously. Any resemblance to actual persons, living or dead, events, or locales is entirely coincidental.

Copyright © 2022 by Stephanie Jones

All rights reserved. No part of this book may be reproduced or used in any manner without written permission of the copyright owner except for the use of quotations in a book review. For more information, address: info@malindi.co.uk

First paperback edition October 2022

Book design by Stephen Jones
Illustrations by Stephen Jones

ISBNs:
978-1-80227-898-9 (Paperback)
978-1-80227-899-6 (eBook)

www.malindi.co.uk

Contents

FOREWORD ix

Chapter 1   HUMAN RELATIONSHIPS 1

Chapter 2   RELATED FAMILY 11

Chapter 3   NON-RELATED FAMILY 23

Chapter 4   FRIENDS 33

Chapter 5   OTHER PEOPLE 41

Chapter 6   WHAT ARE OTHERS CAPABLE OF 51

Chapter 7   HURT 53

Chapter 8   REACTIVE HEALING 55

Chapter 9   CARE 57

Chapter 10   EXERCISE TO AID RELEASE OF SUPPRESSED EMOTIONAL INFORMATION 59

Chapter 11   REALISATION 63

IN SUMMARY 67

DEDICATION

To All People Everywhere

"Words have the power to both destroy and heal
When words are both true and kind, they can change
our world."

– *Buddha*

FOREWORD

Emotions are bread and butter to our Soul.

They are at a level of our being to which we all subscribe and succumb to because of our very makeup.

However, we are nothing without our emotions, as they are how we now respond to past conditioning by others. Becoming aware of them helps us to release past negatives and traumas which lets us then move forward healthier in Mind, Body and Soul.

This book is merely an observation and a short look, by myself, at some ways in which, I feel, we may have been groomed for Life. Some ways that hurt us and some that uplift us.

Our emotional reactions play a very big part in how we conduct our lives.

We can choose to fully interact to whirl and swirl each day into worry, anger and pain or with some effort, choose to detach slightly out of the whirls and swirls and let them get on without us.

What can we learn and how can we become tolerant of ourselves and each other without judgement or enclosing or smothering any relationship?

It is possible to use this book as your own personal workbook because as you read through you will be asked questions which will hopefully, provoke thought and reactions.

Get pen and paper ready.

There are spaces in this book to use and fill in your answers.

Please try this.

Chapter 1

HUMAN RELATIONSHIPS

SELF:

Negatives:

You are the hardest of all to relate to and yet without doing this there is little way forward out of any present situation.

You can be so ready to be 'down 'on yourself, be lacking in grace and gratitude. Feeling there is no joy left in your life, it becomes a drudge to dread.

Being tough on yourself becomes an attitude and is soon accepted as being normal. 'I can do anything, be anyone, and be anywhere.' You can seem to be all things to all people and play the roles without thinking, being reactive to both negative and positive responses during your day. These fuel your day. Eventually, enough is enough, you feel drained and tired all the time with illness and dis-ease creeping in more often.

Take some time to sit and reflect on how you treat yourself.

Do you feel frustrated with lack of reciprocal caring?

Do others take you for granted?

Do you take some time away from your busy schedule of life to amuse yourself in a happy and caring way? E.g. A hobby, walking, exercise.

Do you feel at others beck and call at any time, day or night?

Are you tired most of the time?

Have you developed a body or mind illness and have to cope yourself?

These are just a few of the things that come from lack of self-esteem and confidence in yourself.

SELF:

Positives:

You can change your Life. Have no doubts about this statement.

Self-analysis can be key to moving out of a victim role and finding the confidence to be yourself.

You may need some help but just by the asking for it is a great realisation of the truth that you actually do need help.

You can ask yourself what has led you to this awareness that you need a change, with some help along the way, to do so.

By making some efforts, there is always a shift in attitude and aptitude.

We can begin by asking some questions of ourselves. This is always a good idea as self-analysis can help enormously.

So let's begin:

Where do you think changes need to be made?

What changes do you feel you can facilitate now?

Who do you think will benefit?

There is nothing more glorious than a person coming into joyful awareness that they are worthy of love and friendship.

Their eyes shine with a greater depth and their face lights up with more relaxation of the dislike once felt for the Self.

Confident and animated speech takes the place of silence and lack of self-esteem.

Passion and zest for life takes over once more, or, as we say in Wales, 'Hwyl'.

PARTNER/S:

This area can be an emotional minefield and is the next hardest condition to understand and move forward from.

A. How often do we hear that we can use a relationship as a security blanket?

This can mean that either or both partner can be living a lie in that there is no love left or the relationship has shrivelled to the daily niceties and being courteous.

The partnership becomes a convenience to each for various reasons, possibly as follows: *The consideration of other house members becomes paramount:*

There may be children to consider or perhaps elderly parents being cared for.

Either way, the reason for being together, love, is not there anymore.

B. Perhaps one or both in the relationship is having an outside relationship:

This is such a common but important factor which affects behaviour and emotions on both sides of the partnership in a way that could cause shrugged shoulders and 'a let's get on with life attitude - just be as we are.'
That's the easy option but does not usually happen.

What usually happens is a prolific wave of emotions, sometimes all the following, sometimes some of them. Human nature is monogamous by default and as it can then be assumed that a partner is there for life, the other person is treated with that mindset.

One partner, or both, if suited, can be held in loving affection and esteem for a short while or a long time, but usually this is not sustainable. Little rifts and faults begin to show in another's character which can irritate and displease.

Someone else comes into the frame and shines a light on the situation and it then becomes intolerable.

The truth of the situation is seen through another's eyes.

Then **it** starts, the negative tirades:

    Jealousy,
    Anger,
    Unreasonable behaviour,
    Mistrust,
    Verbal abuse,
    Physical abuse,
    Coldness,
    Couldn't care less attitude,
    Becoming withdrawn
    Do as you want,
    Withdrawal of money,
    Non-payment of bills,
    Over reacting,
    Threatening behaviour with the child or children, other family members.

Spending more time away from home without explanation.

None of these are good situations and leaves much scarring of the whole self.

However, if we are willing to embrace change and believe that all that has happened to us has happened for very good reasons, then we can move forward and make a difference.

It's about being aware and needing to make change that is important-it does not matter how small the change is, any start made will lead to a better life.

It may not be easy for you but try to be very honest with your feelings and answer the following questions in a truthful and direct way.

This is a cathartic way to recall the hurt and the anger that you may have felt.

Just let it happen and flow, then write down your feelings.

There are questions after each section.

Have you had any similar experiences like this?

What did you do?

What can you do to make a change?

Are you afraid to make a change?

C. Perhaps one or both in the relationship has had an outside relationship:

There may be jealousy and anger caused by a past outside relationship that is hard to forgive and overcome. That is a very difficult situation as it leaves a very sour taste in the heart with little understanding. A loss of esteem and confidence is felt by the partner who feels the victim.

It can be that you feel you strongly love another person and not be responded to.

Perhaps you truly loved this person at one time?

Is it the same for you? Really?

Are you feeling inadequate and unloved, used and battered by words, deeds and / or actions?

Is this real love anyway? Ask yourself.

Are you being emotionally blackmailed or is this an emotional comfort blanket?

Is it time to do something positive for yourself?

Emotions are not meant to make us feel lesser persons than others, making us feel down and despondent. See it for what it says, e-motions, just like e-mails, say it, then let it go!

We can get into a habit of feeling the same every day, going through the same motions and reactions to our feelings of guilt and lack of self-esteem. It can be changed.

Has this happened to you?

How did it work out?

Is life more tolerable or is it at an impasse?

D. You can be truly loved by your partner but not feel the same way.

This may be a situation which may feel suffocating and stifling which is not, of course, a pleasant way to live.

There may have been a sense of duty or gratitude to the partner at one time which does not always allow a permanent feeling of happiness.

A sense of duty soon wears off leaving you wanting to flee, to be free, to roam and have adventures. This is a normal reaction and it takes an open couple relationship to talk this through and allow it to work.

Has this happened to you?

Have you resolved anything with your partner?

How are the children now, if any?

Chapter 2

RELATED FAMILY

I would like to say, dear Reader, say that the following questions are not designed to hurt you or to be inconsiderate to your feelings.

If you feel they are, I apologise to you unreservedly.

These questions are here to help reach into your memory and emotions to ascertain your feelings and aid your recognition as to what roles we each have in each other's lives.

I believe it is only then that you can help yourself to move forward to a more joyful life using the knowledge gained from experiences you yourself have manifested in your life to date.

This is a self-analysis programme and can aid the release of pent-up feelings of hurt and lack of self-esteem. These are blocks to a fulfilling and enjoyable life.

A clearer release and download of your own information are supportive to your emotions and mental health.

Your psychological aspect will benefit as clarity and honesty will dissolve the withholding of the fears and frustrations that have built up over the years.

Please write down answers to the questions as you go. With this approach it will ensure a fresh, spontaneous and truthful answer.

Maternal Great Grandmother and Great Grandfather

Are they still alive?

If so, in what way have they contributed to your life?

Have they been active in your upbringing?

If not alive, what do you remember about them?

What do they mean to you now?

Paternal Great Grandmother and Great Grandfather

The same questions will be pertinent as to your Maternal Great Grandparents.

Are they still alive?
If so, in what way have they contributed to your life?

Have they been active in your upbringing?

If not alive, what do you remember about them?

What do they mean to you now?

Maternal Grandmother and Grandfather

Are they still alive?

If so, in what way have they contributed to your life?

Have they been active in your upbringing?

If not alive, what do you remember about them?

What do they mean to you now?

Paternal Grandmother and Grandfather

Are they still alive?

If so, in what way have they contributed to your life?

Have they been active in your upbringing?

If not alive, what do you remember about them?

What do they mean to you now?

Mother

Is she still alive?

If so, in what way do you think she contributed to your life?

Was she active in your upbringing?

If not alive, what do you remember about her?

What does she mean to you now?

Father

Is he still alive?

If so, in what way did he contribute to your life?

Had he been active in your upbringing?

If he is not alive, what do you remember about him?

What does he mean to you now?

Sisters and partners

Is she or are they still alive?

If so, in what way did she or they contribute to your life?

Has she or they been active in your upbringing?

If not alive, what do you remember about her or them?

What does she or they mean to you now?

Brothers and partners

Is he or are they still alive?

If so, in what way has he or they contributed to your life?

Has he or they been active in your upbringing?

If not alive, what do you remember about him or them?

What does he or they mean to you now?

Daughters and partners

Is she or are they still alive?

If so, in what way has she or they contributed to your life?

If not alive, what do you remember about her or them?

What does she or they mean to you now?

Sons and partners

Is he or are they still alive?

If so, in what way has he or they contributed to your life?

If not alive, what do you remember about him or them?

What do they mean to you now?

Granddaughter and partners

Is she or are they still alive?

If so, in what way has she or they contributed to your life?

If not alive, what do you remember about her or them?

What do they mean to you now?

Grandsons and partners

Is he or are they still alive?

If so, in what way has he or they contributed to your life?

If not alive, what do you remember about him or them?

What do they mean to you now?

Aunts and partners

Is she or are they still alive?

If so, in what way has she or they contributed to your life?

Has she or they been active in your upbringing?

If not alive, what do you remember about her or them?

What do they mean to you now?

Uncles and partners

Is he or are they still alive?

If so, in what has he or they contributed to your life?

Has he or they been active in your upbringing?

If not alive, what do you remember about him or them?

What do they mean to you now?

Cousins and partners

Are they still alive?

If so, how and what have they contributed to your life?

Have they been active in your upbringing?

If not alive, what do you remember about them?

What do they mean to you now?

Nieces and partners

Is she or are they still alive?

If so, how and what has she or they contributed to your life?

Has she or they been active in your upbringing?

If not alive, what do you remember about her or them?

What does she or they mean to you now?

Nephews and partners

Is he or are they still alive?

If so, what has he or they contributed to your life?

Has he or they been active in your upbringing?

If not alive, what do you remember about him or them?

What do they mean to you now?

CHAPTER 3

NON-RELATED FAMILY

I feel that these situations are very poignant ones, in that a conscious decision has been made to accept another person's baby or child/children into your life and home to look after and care for them as if they were your own.

There may have been many emotive and emotional issues before this decision was decided upon with much heart searching for a couple or a single person to take this step in giving a home.

There are rigorous restrictions and regulations in place by authorities all over the UK and the persons who wish to care for a child or children in this way have to confront many testing interviews and be open to questioning about all areas in life.

Authorities now have many rules about who can be accepted for this important role and in what manner.

One day, hopefully, it will be seen as a very powerful message to the child and others that are taken in, that to go through all the hoops and regulations the parent or parents were required to make, not only shows them how much they were wanted but how much they were loved. The love was given naturally and freely.

Many children go through life with their natural parents or parent but experiences show that a similar level of love and nurturing is not guaranteed.

Some could argue that this way of accepting a child into the family is more loving and accepting of parenthood than those who have children freely without planning them.

A point to ponder.

Parent/s to Adopted child/children

Arguably, this is the situation that pulls the heart strings the most. Why do I say that?
There can be several reasons:

A. Well usually, the couple or single parent has a difficulty to conceive.

This could be a physical condition which does not allow the fertility necessary to create an egg in the womb.

B. It could be due to the man or woman who usually have been trying for a baby for years with no success. This causes heartache and frustration and look to adopt a stranger's baby or child.

C. A family member has died leaving children behind. There seems no other alternative but to be welcomed into a family they know. Sometimes this leads to adoption to give the child a good family base and familiarity after trauma of losing a parent or perhaps even both parents.

The relationship with these parents are basically the same as with natural parents but one day, usually, the adopting parents tell the child that they have been adopted into the Family and are not the natural birth parents.

What would that mean to the child?

Your Adopted Mother

Is she still alive?

If so, in what way do you think she contributed to your life?

Was she active in your upbringing?

If not alive, what do you remember about her?

What does she mean to you now?

About Your Birth Mother

What do you feel about her?

Is she still alive?

Have you tried to contact her?

If so, what was the outcome?

Your Adopted Father

Is he still alive?

If so, in what way do you think he contributed to your life?

Was he active in your upbringing?

If not alive, what do you remember about him?

What does he mean to you now?

About Your Birth Father

What do you feel about him?

Is he still alive?

Have you tried to contact him?

If so, what was the outcome?

Guardianship of child/children

There are varied reasons why a person or persons would become Guardian over a child/children.

This means they have a legal responsibility to look after the child/children until they are of age to leave home. Sometimes it is for financial reasons.

It usually involves the authorities and the courts to decide if a person/s responsible enough to look after a child.

It does not always mean that a family member steps in to act as guardian but, this can happen depending on circumstances surrounding the case. There may be no other family member able to step in.

About your Guardian

Did you have a Guardian?

Mother or Father figure?

How was your relationship with them?

Did they care for you or was it a financial arrangement?

Foster Parent to child/children

In many ways this is a selfless, caring way that responsible adults show to children who have been removed from parents incapable of their care and affection. Many reasons again. Foster parents give a child/children a home environment, inviting them to share in a family supporting unit. This could be for a short or extended stay depending on circumstances surrounding the judicial decisions made for the welfare of the child/children.

The foster parents apply to the local authorities for this temporary parenting position, usually being able to offer love and attention for the well being of the child/children. After gruelling and exhaustive investigation of their background and character, the foster parent/s are either granted this key role or fails. It must be said that authorities usually pay towards the costs of housing, food and nurturing the child/children while they are in their care. Nevertheless, they are usually special caring people who can give a child/children a foundation of family life until a more permanent position is found. When this happens, the process for them starts again, to be granted temporary custody. Foster parents are transients in a child's/children's life/lives able to make a sacrifice for the welfare of a child/ children. Although un-related they have the ability and opportunity to provide a safe haven for the child/children of any age, from birth to teens, while their future is contemplated and decided upon.

This is emotionally difficult and unenviable work, but foster parents show open heartedness and durability for the long run of the lives they assist and care for.

About your Foster Mother

Did you have a Foster Mother?

If so, in what way do you think she contributed to your life?

Was she active in your upbringing?

What do you remember about her?

What does she mean to you now?

About your Foster Father

Did you have a Foster Father?

If so, in what way do you think he contributed to your life?

Was he active in your upbringing?

What do you remember about him?

What does he mean to you now?

Surrogate parent to others' child/children

There are two platforms from which to view this issue. Like two sides of a coin.

1. On one side we have the Surrogate Mother

This is a woman who agrees to have another couple's baby for them due to physical difficulties. This can be for a couple or a single person.

How this works out over long term is very much down to the psychological aspect and emotional maturity and awareness of the surrogate Mother. It can never be easy to give away a child after it has been nurtured in the womb: feelings and emotions come very much into play.

2. On the other side we have the recipients of the surrogated baby.

A single person or a gay couple have a right to a choice whether to have a surrogate family. They are really needing to have a family but due to circumstances is not possible on their own but have to find a surrogate mother to have their baby for them. Strictly speaking, of course, this is not an adoption

CHAPTER 4

FRIENDS

Very Close Friends

These people are instant friends and can come along at any age or stage of our life. They can be friends who were made at a very young age at school; some are made later along the way during life, through work, hobbies and sports. They are our Soul family like our brothers or sisters, but the relationship can be more intense, loyal and open.

They can instantly recognise you as part of them and there is a comfortable, intimate feeling straight away.

You can talk to them about anything and they will support you, not judge you.

They accept you for who you are without exception.

You know who they are without exception.

You can usually count your very close friends on the fingers of one hand, possibly two hands, if you are very fortunate.

Positive Emotional State

They can be your emotional crutch, in an effective and supportive way. There is nothing you cannot share with them. They then help you to feel better and see the wider picture of any challenges and illnesses you have fallen into. They may be called our 'Guardian Angels 'or 'Earth Angels'.

Being close to you they can be very honest and let you know exactly how you are behaving or reacting to emotional situations. They are your safety valves to let off steam with and to keep you sane. Everyone should have a guardian angel on earth like this.

The positive aspects are immense and they will comfort and support offering the benefits of their own experiences, whether good or bad. They will motivate you at times to keep going, no matter what. They will laugh with you, cry with you, mourn with you, and celebrate with you, sharing the good times and the bad times. You may sometimes never see them for years, they may move away to foreign lands. However, the friendship and closeness is a fact and will remain for life between you.

Negative Emotional State

Sometimes, fallouts and differences of opinions can, and do, occur when someone crosses the line of friendly integrity. This is where a beautifully close friendship can falter and even wither away. Never to return. The emotional strain will be hard to bear and there may be serious effects to follow. The negative aspects of a fallen friendship can be hard to bear.

Bitterness and rivalry can be induced and sustained in cases like these because the intimate knowledge of each other's weaknesses provides a sharp edge sword with which to attack and defend.

GOOD FRIENDS

It is possible to have many friends usually and they are around for social events and gatherings.

These are people who have known you, either for a short time or possibly longer and have become friends because you have things in common.

Positive Emotional State

They will encourage you to be more social and to help get you out of yourself. If you are feeling down or are ill then they will lend a practical hand to help you on your way. They are not generally your confidants, preferring mostly to dip in and out of your life without becoming too attached.

Negative Emotional State

I have experienced this and am able to now detach and see it for what it is. It concerns a very good friend of mine, who had been in my life since I was about twenty years old. I had recently married and moved away to a new area in Wales. This was a whole new start to a whole new way of life. There was so much to look forward to. I have never found it easy to make new friends and this is still the case. However, when one is young an effort is made and it can seem easier to join hobby clubs and socialise! I did this and my husband and I befriended another young couple and we spent a lot of social time together. We became good friends and became part of each other's family.

Eventually, a house move came on the horizon for my friend and she and her husband moved away. Co-incidentally, a move came for me and my husband soon after and we ended up near our friends! This happened a few times over some years and it was often joked about. My friend is a lovely, open and generous person with a lively personality which I loved.

Over the years we were still good friends but not of the close type of friendship which came with a very close friend. Who knows why it was this way?

This is in the negative state category because we have now lost touch over an emotional crisis. Her husband died and we all moved apart. Strange how life works. What was the glue holding us together? I believe it is still a valuable friendship and know that she is still out there and loves her own family.

ACQUAINTANCES

Through a hobby, at the doctors, dentists surgeries, anywhere outside the home where people gather

Positive Emotional State

It gives great satisfaction to know that people can meet outside the home and forge a ring of acquaintances that have nothing to do with knowing you or your life in any sort of depth.

This can be both a positive and a negative state depending on how you view it whether as a social requirement or need. To speak to others, to relate to the challenges others and the self are having. This can keep us in the 'now' and to even accept our own challenges as being miniscule because of hearing others greater difficulties. Positively, acquaintances restore our faith in our ability to befriend others and be social.

This interaction only goes as far as you want it to go and the control is generally in your own hands.

Sometimes, it becomes a ritual to see the same people at the same place at the same time, saying the same things each time.

It can imply no commitment to any relationship.

Being part of a group, requiring assistance and a service of some sort can ease the pressure and take the mind away from troubles, temporarily.

Negative Emotional State

A person can feel there is no need for other people in their life due to various reasons encouraging the feelings and the need to be alone, which in turn encourages a 'lost' feeling. There may have been a bereavement: the loss of a loved one maybe

They may be ill and depressed.

They may be distracted by stress at home or at work.

There are other reasons also; you may add your own, here:

By holding these states of mind, a person does not usually interact with acquaintances met outside the home.

Because it is not necessary to communicate with them, there is no nurturing being interacted. The loneliness factor is promoted within and projected outwardly.

The need for friendship and camaraderie is pushed away.

There is no responsibility to share feelings and thoughts.

It is thought to be easier to negotiate problems when there is no requirement to share feelings. This negative state of mind can allow feelings of social inadequacies to fester and manifest as antisocial. Sometimes this is not what was wanted or needed. It takes time then to readdress this and adjust the cause and effect to harmony.

SHOPPING TRIPS

Shopping trips are generally an essential part of everyone's life. Whether married or single, male or female this is a need that fulfils a role in society. It can be a social family trip or carried out solely at any time. It doesn't really matter as long as it can be part of a daily or weekly ritual to stock up the store cupboards, keep up to date with new shopping items and trends. Healthier eating habits can be experimented with, thereby keeping an interest in food and drink and good health becomes imperative.

Positive Emotional State

It is obvious that we need to shop, whether it is for food, clothes, necessary daily items or luxuries. There is an aspect of spending money that can be very satisfying and helps to make you feel like a provider! This goes way back to cave-man days when man brought home the food and other possible things to use for clothes and fire, just basics to live really. We have taken all this to a very different level, now that we are 'civilised'. Now it is mostly women that do the shopping and it is either for the basics, on a budget, or spending money on short term luxuries. There are such a variety of clothes and other unnecessary items that it can be very satisfying to the ego to be able to afford things that are seen by others to be a little bit better. These days there are many attractions and temptations to take us off the tracks. Feeling good, being able to provide for self and family is paramount to allow stability. New creative hobbies can arise such as cooking and sewing, which enhances well-being and satisfaction within a family. All members of a family can be included which is ideal to bond with each other over similar interests.

Negative Emotional State

Unfortunately, there is a down side to everything. While shopping can be seen as a necessity in so many ways, it can also be used as an emotional crutch. What I mean is that it becomes an addiction to compensate for some shortcoming in a person's life. This could be:

Unhappiness in a partner relationship, or
Unhappiness in a relationship with oneself.

Money becomes a vehicle to hide depression and loneliness by buying goods which are wanted but not necessary. Goods will be purchased if something takes the eye, but not always needed. Many things are purchased regardless of whether money is available. Credit cards are used, and their limits reached and exceeded. Items may be used once then are usually stored at home unused. There are usually signs of this in a person's house when everything can appear new and fresh.

So many levels are reached of unease and emptiness. If not assisted, it can escalate into huge proportions ruining lives. Take note of these points and if you see something within yourself or a close one, try to take steps to change. Judgement is not required, only loving, helpful support and maybe outside professional help.

Do you see any addictive tendencies in yourself?

If so, what are they? Please be honest, only you are reading the answers,

What steps can you take to make change?

Do you recognise a relationship is involved?

Can a professional help? Such as your GP or Social Services?

CHAPTER 5

OTHER PEOPLE

Colleagues at Work

Positive Emotional State

As we spend a large part of our working life being with others in the workplace it is important to feel we are accepted and respected for the work we do. This can be down to having a knowledgeable and understanding boss or head of section. It can also be attributed to having supportive and not over- friendly work colleagues who attend to their own work and business, not interfering in your work in any way. They can be supportive of ideas and help to implement beneficial changes which aid everyone's peace of mind and can increase productivity.

At the end of each working day there is a camaraderie and good-natured goodnight before leaving for home.

A good day encourages good vibes for all.

Everyone is happy. This is, of course, an ideal situation and something to aspire to!

Negative Emotional State

If a colleague or, perhaps, a boss, at work makes your life difficult for you while at work, then your whole life, both inside and outside of work can become emotionally charged with the pressure leading to illness and stress. Everything and everyone near you suffers the same as you as you are unable to see past it to a harmonious solution.

I had such an experience with a boss, who was a manager, at my place of work, who was transferred in from another office in England. He was a high flyer who was gathering notches to put in his CV. I was an easy target, I suppose. He thought I was inefficient or ineffective at my work. Just why he thought that I never got to know the truth of it: other than to admit one time that he didn't like me.

His approach and mine were very different to our work, I got results my way and he in his way. I have to admit that I didn't like him either. It was a two way street. I really hated going in to work every day, just knowing he was in his office made me fearful and angry with him and myself for feeling that way.

How is it that some people have this effect over you when you know you are successful in your way and reaching targets set? I had nothing really to worry about other than he had power over me to make my life miserable and could have me transferred out to another office if he chose to. Indeed, he did threaten this once. My whole life became an angry emotional mess. Every one suffered around me at home. I couldn't sleep or eat properly through worry of the next day ahead. This went on for nearly a year and I was a wreck.

The universe sorted it for me and must have decided I had had enough! He had done his time in my office and was transferred out to a cushy job overseas in lots of sunshine. Was I glad!? Of course, I even contributed to his farewell gift to get rid of him.

It does not sound very good hearted to say these things but I want to show that experiences like this do happen and happen to those people who are undeserving of hurt and pain and misery. Such, however, is the way of Life. I learned many lessons from this man and am grateful to have had the opportunity of gaining such wisdom. We did say goodbye to each other but he was flippant. I am more serious and it took me many years to clear his unhappiness and shortcomings from me. Eventually, I helped him on his way in peace. I give him no power over me anymore. I now give him no thought other than to illuminate him as an example in this book.

At Play

In order to balance our busy lives, there needs to be an element of fun, play, if you like to call it that. This can take the forms of hobbies, exercise, spiritual practices such as meditation, yoga, re-living a passion for subjects close to your heart such as subjective reading, singing, caring for others, perhaps volunteering to assist in places or areas you have knowledge or interest in.

Positive Emotional State

While we are attending to our own enjoyment it seems we meet others of like minds, another aspect of enjoyment and life balance. We not only meet teachers but seekers of knowledge and community. When we can allow and free ourselves to join in, there are many benefits that make our hearts sing. We learn to share, to trust, to support. We each have something to contribute in the way of empathy through similar life experiences and we each draw on this empathy creating a safe and loving environment which is richer because we allowed ourselves to 'play' and share.

Negative Emotional State

Of course, we realise life is not always a wonderfully positive place that allows us to sing happily every day and night. There are what are called 'tests', which are emotionally challenging and hurtful.

How these 'tests' come about is thought provoking and can seem unfair and untimely. Usually happening when things are swinging along quite nicely for a change! There can be down sides to our aspect of 'play' due to the fact that we can expect too much of ourselves and others. Getting out and about takes a lot of courage for some people who have been housebound for varied reasons. It is not easy to 'play', indeed, it may be that the thought of it being 'play' is a deterrent. So, when new hobbies and interests are sourced and begun it can be innocently felt that everyone will be accepting, open and helpful. That is not always the case and may lead to frustration and hurtful neglect or abuse of one's abilities.

Also, even when people have been pursuing leisure activities for a while, there can become an element of competition and feelings of inadequacy. Play is not always an answer to a more fulfilling life, but it remains that we must find the right activities for ourselves and enjoy.

Other People:

In service to you:

This could be anywhere: at the garage, shops, or by professionals such as doctors, dentists, therapists

Positive Emotional State

Trust is the requirement here to reach a positive emotional outcome. As professionals in service there is a perception that all are knowledgeable, capable and understanding of their own specialities. Some people have complete faith in their abilities and receive the best of care and attention and some don't. Those that do may achieve wellness and satisfaction in different forms. It is true that when you give respect you may generally expect to receive it.

I remember breaking down in my car on a very lonely main road late at night. I walked to the nearest phone box with trepidation and rang the RAC. They came within half an hour, put me at my ease, repaired my car and I was on my way within an hour of breaking down. Such was my relief, I stayed with the RAC ever since. Loyalty was the outcome together with emotional relief that I had not come to any harm or danger while at the roadside. I knew help was coming along and it did.

Of course, this is only one scenario, there are so many more. Can you recall a situation which had a positive outcome, to your relief?

Write it here...

Negative Emotional State

Long ago, a dentist looked into my mouth and he said, "I think we should take that tooth out today". I was out of that dentists chair faster than you could call my name and I never went back for many many years to any dentist. What had he done to me that was negative? Why, he was going to wrench out a part of me. I already had a distaste of dentists and their surgically smelling surgeries and efficient nurses, not through many experiences but through the stories I had heard from my school friends of their experiences.

I remember going home and not telling my parents that I had chickened out so drastically as I knew they would drag me back! I was only eleven. I was fearful and it took me a long time to recognise that it was me and not the dentist who had the power of fear over me.

It was many decades before I drew on my own power, faced my fear and found a dentist who understood my problems and was kindly. To be fair, this is more the norm these days as part of their training is to empathise and understand how people might be truly afraid and of how to deal with it.

Did you have a negative experience you would care to recall here?

Write it here...

You in Service to Others:

You may be in a service industry yourself, or in a caring role perhaps.

Positive Emotional State

This gives a feel-good effect. Whether you are very young or much older, this caring role can be the best. It can keep in touch with all human frailties and challenges restoring strength, trust, and self-belief and self- responsibility. By helping others, we can help ourselves too.

Giving is not a requirement or entitlement to receive but to see others and appreciate the help and attention you give can be enormously satisfying.

You may be a family member caring for another family member, friend, relative or a stranger.

You may be a professional carer being paid to help another.

You may be a doctor or other qualified professional such as a Therapist.

What do you do?

Are you in a caring role?

What are the positives you feel?
Write here ...

Negative Emotional State

Being in a caring role, of any kind, we can care too much, love too much, worry too much, pamper and cosset too much. These can be inappropriate after a while and a sense of frustration and anger can creep in. When we are held back in our own lives and needs we pull away leaving disappointment and perhaps anger, behind. It is not easy to cope with all the stresses and worries that caring for another can bring. This applies to animals as well as fellow humans. There seems to be no cut-off point as to where over-care comes in and the balance of mind, heart and body is adversely affected. When it is realised what is happening and lives are affected, it can be too late to re-address the balance and harmony regained.

This may or may not be easier for a professional who needs to learn to leave the 'troubles' behind when they return home at the end of a busy day. This is not always accomplished and professional de-briefing aftercare, is given by a colleague with similar work and experience.

The family member who gives care is not as fortunate. Who is there to give a professional de-briefing after a stressful day fraught with worries, physical activities causing drop down tiredness? This can be experienced as being caught in a trap with no-one to help, a cry in the dark. Luckily, if the strength to ask for help is there, then it can be offered. But usually, people cope alone, feeling out of the human race and trapped. There is always a choice, open your heart, and ask for help.

Do you need help?

Write here.......

Given the human susceptibility for trauma, it is not difficult to sense or experience the heartaches that surround every experience, be it illness, death, divorce, moving to a new house, changing jobs, disappointments, first love, first job, parental responsibilities.

There are many more, can you add any?

Write here.....

CHAPTER 6

WHAT ARE OTHERS CAPABLE OF

Positives:

- Care
- Love
- Support
- Boost ego and pride
- Encouragement
- Being humorous
- Validating the importance of self
- Defend against injustices
- Allow self development

Negatives:

- Hurt
- Anger
- Psychological abuse. e.g. mind games
- Physical abuse
- Disappointment
- Reduce self esteem
- Irrational behaviour
- Blaming culture
- Undermining your authority with others
- Emotional entrapment
- Spiritual depravation

Unsupportive
Controlling
Guilt

Can you name more?

CHAPTER 7

HURT

Some things we say which are designed to hurt:

I hate you
I can't stand you
Get a life
Don't wear your heart on your sleeve
Keep yourself to yourself
Don't be silly
You smell
You're no good
Why can't you be like him/her?
What do you think you're doing?
Get away from me
I'm not interested
What makes you think you can do that?
Ha-ha, did you do that?
You have no colour sense
You dress like a tart
Your hair looks awful
Get something done to yourself
You'll never do that
Don't tell anyone
I am going on my own
I trusted you
You don't listen to me
I won't hear what you are saying
Who do you think you are?

No one will believe you
What do you do all day?
I/we will be better off without you

Can you add some of your own from your own experiences?
It will be cathartic to do this little exercise.

Why do these remarks have such an effect on us?

Why do we allow people to have an impact on what we do and why we do it?

What are the reasons behind these comments that another person makes

Why do these comments become triggers for an emotional disturbance?

Is there a way to react without becoming emotional and upset?

CHAPTER 8

REACTIVE HEALING

Reactive Healing is the answer

Help yourself to understand yourself
Become tired of being the victim
Tell yourself you are no one's puppet
Allow some leeway with your thinking that you have to be perfect all the time, this is impossible
Look at your situation in life and ask yourself if it agrees with you
Are you ill a lot of the time with various ailments, whether acute or chronic? And, if so, do you feel these are self-induced?
Do you know or feel that you can have a different life and change the one you have?
Cast your mind back to when you were younger and revisit the aims and dreams you had. Have you wandered a long way from that path?
Make a promise to yourself that you will endeavour to return to the innocent and childlike person you were many years ago before Life became harder.
Is it really difficult to be yourself? You may have forgotten or blocked out more nurturing times: sadly, perhaps you didn't have any.
If you are fortunate to have a very close or good friend, talk to them about your fears and dislikes: how you have arrived at this low point in your life. It won't

be easy but it will be cathartic when you can release without being judged.

Not having a friend to talk to does not make this situation impossible. You can perhaps seek out a relative or someone you can even pay on a professional basis to listen to you. That's all it takes: someone to listen while you untangle yourself from the jungle of problems and emotional upsets which have caught you like a fish in a net.

Being reactive in your distress will help you to move forward positively, even if it does seem, initially, like walking through treacle!

By helping yourself to help yourself, will give you the knowing that you do have the courage and strength to come out of your misery: it will lead to higher self esteem and confidence.

Write down how you can make a start to reactive healing.

CHAPTER 9

CARE

Some things we say which are designed to show we care:

I love you
That's really good
Well done
How lovely you look today
Just had your hair done?
You look good in that
You are a caring person
You can do that
It's something you can do
You always try your best
No pressure
Come with me
I love it when you are with me
You make everyone feel special, me too
What a lovely smile
Thank you for being you
I love you as you are
The family is nothing without you
I miss you
Home is where my heart is if you are there
Let's do it together

Can you add some sayings you say or others have said to you in your own experiences?
It will be cathartic to do this little exercise.

CHAPTER 10

Exercise to Aid Release of Suppressed Emotional Information

Please answer the questions and write down your answers in the space provided.

1) *Is there a person, in your own life, that you recall as having the most influence on your life?*

Name this person.

Was this person good for you?

Was this person bad for you?

Is there a phrase highlighted in your mind that they may have repeatedly said to you? E.g. "don't be silly!"

Do you think this has an effect on your present life, what you have become and who you are?

Do you feel this person was being positive or negative toward you?

What are your feelings about their input to your life?

Are you: nourished or satisfied or hurt or encouraged or strengthened or weakened?

How do you feel about this person?

2) Name a second person who you feel had a considerable influence on your life

Name this person.

Was this person good for you?

Was this person bad for you?

EXERCISE TO AID RELEASE OF SUPPRESSED EMOTIONAL INFORMATION

Is there a phrase highlighted in your mind that they may have repeatedly said to you? E.g. "don't be silly!"

Do you think this has an effect on your present life, what you have become and who you are?
   If so, how has it affected you?

Do you feel this person was being positive or negative toward you?

What are your feelings about their input to your life?

Are you: nourished or satisfied or hurt or encouraged or strengthened or weakened?

How do you feel about this person?

CHAPTER 11

REALISATION

The world is full of people who have issues, some more serious than others but all are created by themselves.

Until they self-realise what is going on, they cannot really be helped but possibly guided toward a realisation of sorts.

It mainly comes from within and can happen at any age.

Youths realising their own reality and life forces can become awesome people who not only have a purpose for themselves but can give/ teach/inform others they come into contact with.

We are all beings of light; some lights are dimmer than others and some shine brightly like the stars in the heavens.

Everyone, without exception, knows the light is within him or her but most choose to keep the light dimmed as it takes less effort.

I can wait, there's no rushing required. Be patient in all things and all will be received and accepted.

The physical and sexual aspect of life is necessary to enact as it brings a new world of feelings, emotions and consciousness.

It is a complete sharing of self and body when it is mutually agreed upon, of course. Its positive aspects lift the mind and higher self thereby enriching the soul.

Start to allow the new feelings to become part of being without them taking over or controlling.

To know that there are such pleasurable wonders within the body which take the self to a higher state of being, to feel such joy and rich contentment?

It is really food for the Soul.

Sharing this intimacy with another like mind only serves to double the experience.

Allowing freedom of each other while being there for each other is the aim, surely.

It should not entirely be necessary to force a paper union on the relationship as on a higher plane the union is made and will blend the two together until time for change/growth.

There is no requirement for the negative aspects such as craving – this will only serve to block your energies and stop the flow of universal love to you.

Also, craving leads to a complete blockage of vitality.

It also has the effect of altering the other person's abilities to lead a fulfilling life when craving is directed towards their energetic body.

Because we are all one energy, we should not mis-use the space around us as our feelings and emotions are released into the universe and carried to that place we are thinking of, whether it be physical form such as human, animals, things of earth, trees, flowers. All these are affected by our thoughts.

Loving thoughts will always reverberate and bring back love to you, like a boomerang.

Any negativity within that love will also come back to you. You get back exactly what you send out.

Negatives sides of love are many:

   need,
   craving,
   over-indulgence,

jealousy,
impatience,
longing,
lack of nurturing of the 'self' and the other Soul,
smothering,
anger,
hatred,
laziness,
dishonesty,
lies and deceit,
pain,
excess,
incarceration,
Idolization,
possessiveness.

We are here to do our best in all our endeavours, whether it is washing the floor or caring in the community, bringing up a family or living alone, being rich or being poor, shaping society or homelessness.

Truly unconditional love is both free and freeing.

One is free to love- or not: and others are free to respond- or not.

Intentions and actions are purely directed toward the good of the other, with no ulterior motives.

This gives a good relationship because ego and self-interest do not get in the way.

IN SUMMARY

As a human race we are fundamentally flawed in our perfection.

What do I mean by this?

I can try to explain, that this is my view of that.

We are all connected by energetic magnetic life force. This ensures that nobody needs to physically be alone whatever their life experiences or where their life path leads.

We could be on a desert island with no other human being around but still be surrounded by air, the energy that feeds our breath, ensures we are alive and vibrating our own energy whether we are happy or sad, rich or poor, spiritually connected or not. There is no distinction. All that we do is for our own benefit, whether we like an experience or not. We can be explorers, stay at homes, orators or live in quiet community settings.

Even though physically alone we sense vibrations of all life on the rest of the planet! It has been proved that animals/humans can adapt to new survival skills where necessary, wherever we are. We are the same. We are born with the powerful innate ability to survive, no matter what our life situations. We interact, we have feelings, we have emotions, we have memory, we have a spiritual connection to the divine, all there is: how could we not be less than perfect?

There is another negative aspect to all that which is how we react to each other.

We are not always kind or tolerant to other people whether we know them or not. We have certain prejudices, usually instilled by others and we develop certain ideas about how others need to behave to ourselves and to others.

We are like sponges when we decide to learn and interact negatively or positively.

We are truly awesome beings. We can put our great fragility and power to good and positive use by helping Mankind to see and feel the positive in all things.

Let us all be kind, tolerant and say positive things to each other.

This is how we can change the world.

www.ingramcontent.com/pod-product-compliance
Lightning Source LLC
Chambersburg PA
CBHW081626100526
44590CB00021B/3616